GROWTH INVESTING

The Beginners Guide To Growth Investing

Benjamin Mornington

Cover design by: Art Painter
Library of Congress Control Number:
Printed in the United States of America

CONTENTS

GROWTH INVESTING

DISCLAIMER

Disclaimer: The author of this book is not a licensed financial professional and the information contained within is not intended to be taken as financial advice. Investing in stocks and other securities carries a risk of loss. Please consult a licensed financial advisor and conduct your own research before making any investment decisions.

It is also important to consult with a tax professional when dealing with tax implications of investing, especially when it comes to reporting, as tax laws and rules may vary depending on the country or state and the circumstances.

ABOUT THE
BOOK

A re you interested in growing your wealth through investing, but don't know where to start? Look no further than "The Beginner's Guide to Growth Investing," a comprehensive guide that will teach you everything you need to know about investing in growth stocks.

In this easy-to-read book, you'll learn the basics of growth investing, including what it is, why it's important, and how to identify growth stocks. You'll also discover how to analyze financial statements and other important metrics to determine if a stock is worth investing in.

But that's not all! "The Beginner's Guide to Growth Investing" also covers more advanced topics such as portfolio diversification, risk management, and market analysis. You'll learn how to create a portfolio that fits your investment goals and risk tolerance, and how to monitor your investments to ensure they continue to perform well.

Whether you're a complete beginner or have some experience with investing, "The Beginner's Guide to Growth Investing" is the perfect resource to help you achieve your financial goals. With clear explanations, helpful examples, and actionable advice, this book will give you the confidence you need to start investing in growth stocks and build your wealth over time.

INTRODUCTION TO GROWTH INVESTING

I nvesting in the stock market is one of the most popular ways to build wealth and achieve financial freedom. But with so many investment strategies and approaches out there, it can be overwhelming to figure out where to start. One approach that has gained popularity in recent years is growth investing.

Growth investing is a strategy that involves investing in companies that are expected to grow at a faster rate than the overall market or their peers. These companies typically reinvest their earnings into the business to fuel future growth, rather than distributing them as dividends to shareholders. The goal of growth investing is to capitalize on the potential for long-term capital appreciation as the company grows and its stock price increases.

But how do you identify a growth company, and what are the risks and rewards of this approach? In this chapter, we'll explore the basics of growth investing and what you need to know to get started.

What is Growth Investing?

Growth investing is a long-term investment strategy that involves investing in companies with the potential for above-average growth in earnings and revenue. Growth companies typically have innovative products or services, strong market positions, and expanding markets. They may also have a competitive advantage in their industry or a strong management team.

The primary goal of growth investing is to generate capital appreciation over the long term. This means that growth investors are less concerned with short-term fluctuations in stock price and more focused on the long-term potential for growth. In many cases, growth companies may not be profitable or may have lower earnings per share than other companies in the same industry, but their potential for future growth justifies their higher valuation.

How to Identify Growth Companies

One of the biggest challenges of growth investing is identifying which companies have the potential for above-average growth. While there is no foolproof method for identifying growth companies, there are several key characteristics that growth investors look for:

1. Innovation: Growth companies are often at the forefront of innovation in their industry, with a focus on developing new products or services that can disrupt the market.

2. Strong market position: Growth companies typically have a strong competitive advantage in their industry, such as a unique product or service, a large market share, or a recognizable brand.

3. Expanding market: Growth companies operate in markets that are expanding, such as emerging industries or growing geographic regions.

4. Financial strength: Growth companies have strong financials, including high revenue growth rates, strong balance sheets, and a history of reinvesting earnings back into the business.

5. Experienced management team: Growth companies have experienced management teams that are focused on long-term growth and have a track record of success.

While these characteristics are not definitive, they can help investors identify companies with the potential for above-average growth.

One of the main advantages of growth investing is the potential for long-term capital appreciation. Growth companies have the potential to grow at a faster rate than the overall market or their peers, which can lead to higher returns over the long term.

Another advantage of growth investing is that growth companies are often less impacted by economic downturns than other companies. This is because growth companies are typically in expanding markets or have a competitive advantage in their industry, which can help them weather economic storms.

Finally, growth investing can be a more exciting and rewarding investment strategy than other approaches. Growth companies are often at the forefront of innovation, and investing in these companies can be a way to support and profit from new technologies and ideas.

DEFINING GROWTH INVESTING

Growth investing is an investment strategy that focuses on investing in companies with the potential for above-average growth in earnings and revenue. This strategy is based on the belief that these companies will outperform the broader market over the long term, as their growth potential leads to higher stock prices.

Growth investors seek out companies that are expected to grow at a faster rate than their peers, based on factors such as expanding markets, innovative products or services, strong market positions, and competitive advantages. These companies may not be profitable or may have lower earnings per share than other companies in the same industry, but their potential for future growth justifies their higher valuation.

Growth investing is a long-term strategy, as it can take time for a company's growth potential to be fully realized. Growth investors are less concerned with short-term fluctuations in stock price and more focused on the long-term potential for growth.

Growth investing is often contrasted with value investing, another popular investment strategy. Value investors seek out companies that are undervalued by the market and have the potential for future growth, based on factors such as strong balance sheets, low price-to-earnings ratios, and high dividend yields.

While both value and growth investing aim to generate long-term returns, they have different approaches to selecting companies. Value investors focus on companies that are trading at a discount to their intrinsic value, while growth investors focus on companies with the potential for above-average growth.

Advantages of Growth Investing

One of the main advantages of growth investing is the potential for long-term capital appreciation. Growth companies have the potential to grow at a faster rate than the overall market or their peers, which can lead to higher returns over the long term.

Another advantage of growth investing is that growth companies are often less impacted by economic downturns than other companies. This is because growth companies are typically in expanding markets or have a competitive advantage in their industry, which can help them weather economic storms.

Finally, growth investing can be a more exciting and rewarding investment strategy than other approaches. Growth companies are often at the forefront of innovation, and investing in these companies can be a way to support and profit from new technologies and ideas.

Risks of Growth Investing

While growth investing can offer many rewards, it is not without risks. One of the main risks of growth investing is that growth companies are often valued at a premium to their peers. This means that their stock prices may already reflect their potential for growth, making it difficult for investors to profit from further growth.

Another risk of growth investing is that growth companies may not meet investors' high expectations for growth. If a growth company fails to live up to its growth potential, its stock price may fall sharply, leading to significant losses for investors.

Finally, growth investing can be more volatile than other investment strategies, as growth companies may experience more significant price swings in response to changes in market conditions or company-specific news.

Growth investing is an investment strategy that

focuses on investing in companies with the potential for above-average growth in earnings and revenue. While growth investing can offer many rewards, it is not without risks. Investors should carefully evaluate the potential risks and rewards of growth investing before making any investment decisions.

HOW TO IDENTIFY GROWTH COMPANIES FOR GROWTH INVESTING

I nvesting in growth companies can be a great way to achieve long-term capital appreciation. Growth companies are businesses that are expected to grow at a faster rate than the overall market or their peers. Identifying growth companies can be a challenging task, but there are several key indicators that investors can look for when evaluating companies. In this article, we'll discuss how to identify growth companies for growth investing.

1. Industry Trends

One way to identify growth companies is to look at the industry trends. Companies operating in industries with expanding markets are more likely to experience growth than those in stagnant or declining industries. For example, companies in the technology sector are often considered growth companies because of the rapid pace of innovation and the increasing demand for technology products and services.

When evaluating industry trends, investors should consider factors such as demographics, consumer behavior, and technological advancements. Companies that are well-positioned to take advantage of these trends are more likely to experience growth in the future.

2. Financial Metrics

Financial metrics can be a useful tool for identifying growth companies. Key financial metrics that investors should look for when evaluating growth companies include revenue growth, earnings growth, and return on equity (ROE).

Revenue growth measures how much a company's sales have increased over time. Investors should look for companies with a history of consistent revenue growth, indicating that their products or services are in high demand.

Earnings growth measures the rate at which a company's profits are increasing. Investors should look for companies with a history of strong earnings growth, indicating that the company is generating healthy profits and has the potential for continued growth in the future.

ROE measures how efficiently a company is using shareholder equity to generate profits. Investors should look for companies with a high ROE, indicating that the company is generating strong returns for its shareholders.

3. Competitive Advantage

Companies with a competitive advantage are more likely to experience growth over the long term. A competitive advantage is what sets a company apart from its peers and makes it a leader in its industry. Companies with a strong competitive advantage are more likely to maintain their market share and continue to grow even as new competitors enter the market.

Investors should look for companies with a unique product or service, a strong brand, or proprietary technology. Companies with a competitive advantage are more likely to maintain their market share and continue to grow even as new competitors enter the market.

4. Management Team

A strong management team is essential for the

success of any company, and it is a key indicator of a growth company. Investors should look for companies with experienced and successful management teams who have a track record of making good business decisions and delivering strong results.

When evaluating a company's management team, investors should consider factors such as the CEO's track record, the experience of the board of directors, and the company's corporate culture. A strong management team can help a company navigate challenges and make strategic decisions that drive long-term growth.

5. Valuation

Finally, investors should consider the valuation of a company when evaluating its growth potential. Growth companies are often valued at a premium to their peers, but investors should ensure that the company's valuation is justified by its growth potential.

Investors should evaluate a company's price-to-earnings (P/E) ratio, price-to-sales (P/S) ratio, and price-to-book (P/B) ratio to determine whether the company is overvalued or undervalued relative to its peers. Companies with high growth potential may justify a higher valuation, but investors should ensure that the valuation is supported by the company's financials and growth prospects.

GROWTH STOCK EXAMPLES

Here are some recent examples (at the time of writing) of good growth stocks from the last 10 years:

Amazon.com Inc

1. Amazon has been one of the most successful growth stocks in recent years, thanks to its enormous and sustained success as an online retailer.

Facebook

2. Facebook has also experienced significant success as a growth company but has faced challenges in recent years due to data privacy and other issues. Despite these setbacks, Facebook continues to be a successful growth stock with a growing user base.

Apple Inc

3. Apple is a highly sought-after growth stock, thanks in part to its loyal consumer base and reputation as a brand consumers want to be associated with. Additionally, Apple's focus on high-quality products and constant innovation gives it a competitive edge over its competitors.

Netflix

4. Netflix is another profitable growth stock, with a loyal and expanding consumer base for its streaming services. As one of the first companies to offer such services, Netflix has enjoyed a competitive advantage over other market participants, allowing it to achieve significant growth.

TOOLS AND RESOURCES FOR FINDING GROWTH STOCKS

Investing in growth stocks requires careful research and analysis to identify companies with the potential for above-average growth in earnings and revenue. Fortunately, there are many tools and resources available to investors to help them find and evaluate growth stocks. In this chapter, we'll explore some of the most useful tools and resources for finding growth stocks.

1. Stock Screeners

Stock screeners are online tools that allow investors to filter stocks based on specific criteria. Stock screeners can be used to identify growth stocks based on metrics such as revenue growth, earnings growth, and price-to-earnings (P/E) ratios. Some popular stock screeners include Finviz, Yahoo Finance, and Google Finance.

Investors can use stock screeners to narrow down their search for growth stocks based on specific criteria, such as industry, market capitalization, and financial metrics. This can help investors save time and focus their research efforts on the most promising growth stocks.

http://finance.yahoo.com

https://www.google.com/finance/

2. Analyst Reports

Analyst reports can provide valuable insights into growth companies and their potential for future growth. Analysts often provide detailed analysis of companies, including financial metrics, market trends, and competitive advantages. Analyst reports can be found on financial news websites, investment research firms, and brokerage websites.

Investors should be cautious when relying on analyst reports, as analysts may have biases or conflicts of interest. It's important to read multiple analyst reports and conduct your own research before making any investment decisions.

3. Industry Reports

Industry reports can provide investors with a comprehensive overview of a specific industry and its potential for growth. Industry reports typically include information on market trends, consumer behavior, and technological advancements. Industry reports can be found on industry association websites, research firms, and financial news websites.

Investors should use industry reports to gain a deeper understanding of the factors driving growth in a specific industry. This can help investors identify growth companies that are well-positioned to take advantage of industry trends and emerging opportunities.

4. Social Media

Social media platforms such as Twitter and LinkedIn can be useful tools for finding growth stocks. Investors can follow industry experts, analysts, and other investors on social media to stay up-to-date on the latest news and trends in their chosen industries. Additionally, investors can join online investment communities to share insights and exchange ideas with other investors.

Investors should use social media as a supplement to other research tools, and should be cautious when relying on information obtained through social media. It's important to verify information and conduct your own research before making any investment decisions.

5. Company Websites and Investor Relations

Company websites and investor relations pages can provide valuable information on a company's financials, growth prospects, and competitive advantages. Investors can review a company's annual reports, investor presentations, and earnings releases to gain insight into its operations and future growth potential.

Investors should review a company's website and investor relations page as part of their due diligence process. It's important to read and understand a company's financials and growth prospects before making any investment decisions.

Finding and evaluating growth stocks requires careful research and analysis. Fortunately, there are many tools and resources available to investors to help them identify and evaluate growth stocks. Investors should use a combination of stock screeners, analyst reports, industry reports, social media, and company websites to conduct thorough research and make informed investment decisions. It's important to conduct your own research and verify information before making any investment decisions.

CRITERIA FOR SELECTING GROWTH STOCKS

G rowth stocks are an attractive investment option for investors who are looking for high potential returns in the long-term. These stocks offer the possibility of higher earnings and revenue growth than their peers and the broader market. However, finding the right growth stocks can be challenging. In this article, we will discuss the criteria for selecting growth stocks.

1. Revenue Growth

One of the most important criteria for selecting growth stocks is revenue growth. A company's revenue growth is a measure of how much its sales have increased over time. Growth stocks are typically companies that are experiencing strong revenue growth, indicating that their products or services are in high demand.

When evaluating revenue growth, investors should look for companies with consistent growth rates over several years. Ideally, a company should have a history of revenue growth of 15% or more annually. However, it's important to note that revenue growth rates can vary by industry, and some industries may have lower growth rates than others.

2. Earnings Growth

Earnings growth is another important criterion for selecting growth stocks. Earnings growth measures the rate at which a company's profits are increasing. Investors should look for companies that have a history of strong earnings growth, indicating that the company is generating healthy profits and has the potential for continued growth in the future.

When evaluating earnings growth, investors should look for companies with a history of consistent earnings growth, as well as positive earnings surprises. Positive earnings surprises occur when a company reports earnings that are higher than analysts' estimates, indicating that the company is performing better than expected.

3. Competitive Advantage

Another key criterion for selecting growth stocks is a company's competitive advantage. A competitive advantage is what sets a company apart from its peers and makes it a leader in its industry. A company with a strong competitive advantage is more likely to continue to grow and generate profits over time.

When evaluating a company's competitive advantage, investors should look for factors such as unique products or services, a strong brand, or proprietary technology. Companies with a competitive advantage are more likely to maintain their market share and continue to grow even as new competitors enter the market.

4. Strong Management Team

A strong management team is essential for the success of any company, and it is a key criterion for selecting growth stocks. Investors should look for companies with experienced and successful management teams who have a track record of making good business decisions and delivering strong results.

When evaluating a company's management team, investors should consider factors such as the CEO's track record, the experience of the board of directors, and the company's corporate culture. A strong management team can help a company navigate challenges and make strategic decisions that drive long-term growth.

5. Financial Strength

Finally, financial strength is an important criterion for selecting growth stocks. Investors should look for companies with a strong balance sheet, low levels of debt, and a history of reinvesting earnings back into the business.

When evaluating a company's financial strength, investors should consider factors such as cash flow, debt-to-equity ratio, and return on equity. Companies with strong financials are more likely to weather economic downturns and continue to invest in their business, which can lead to continued growth and higher stock prices.

Selecting growth stocks can be a challenging process, but by evaluating key criteria such as revenue growth, earnings growth, competitive advantage, strong management team, and financial strength, investors can increase their chances of selecting successful growth stocks. It's important to conduct thorough research and analysis before making any investment decisions, and to consider factors such as risk tolerance and investment goals when selecting growth stocks.

THE DIFFERENCES BETWEEN VALUE, DIVIDEND, AND GROWTH INVESTING

I nvesting in the stock market can be a complex endeavor, with many different strategies and approaches to choose from. Three popular approaches to investing in the stock market are value investing, dividend investing, and growth investing. While all three approaches aim to generate returns for investors, they differ in their investment philosophies and objectives. In this chapter, we'll explore the differences between value, dividend, and growth investing.

Value Investing

Value investing is an investment strategy that seeks out companies that are trading at a discount to their intrinsic value. Intrinsic value is the estimated true value of a company based on its fundamentals, such as earnings, assets, and cash flow. Value investors believe that the market can sometimes undervalue a company, presenting an opportunity to buy the stock at a discount.

Value investors typically look for companies with low price-to-earnings (P/E) ratios, low price-to-book (P/B) ratios, and high dividend yields. These metrics can indicate that a company is undervalued by the market and has the potential for future growth.

The primary objective of value investing is to generate long-term capital appreciation by buying undervalued stocks and holding them until they reach their intrinsic value. Value investors are typically patient and willing to hold onto a stock for several years.

Dividend Investing

Dividend investing is an investment strategy that focuses on companies that pay dividends to their shareholders. Dividends are regular payments made by a company to its shareholders out of its profits or retained earnings. Dividend investors seek out companies with a history of consistent and growing dividend payments, as this can indicate that the company is financially stable and has the potential for future growth.

Dividend investors typically look for companies with high dividend yields, which is the dividend payment as a percentage of the stock price. Companies with high dividend yields are often well-established, stable companies that generate consistent cash flow and profits.

The primary objective of dividend investing is to generate income from regular dividend payments. Dividend investors are typically looking for stable, well-established companies with a history of consistent dividend payments.

Growth Investing

Growth investing is an investment strategy that focuses on companies with the potential for above-average growth in earnings and revenue. Growth companies typically reinvest their earnings back into the business to fuel future growth, rather than distributing them as dividends to shareholders. The goal of growth investing is to capitalize on the potential for long-term capital appreciation as the company grows and its stock price increases.

Growth investors seek out companies that are expected to grow at a faster rate than their peers, based on factors such as expanding markets, innovative products or services, strong market positions, and competitive advantages. These companies may not be profitable or may have lower earnings per share than other companies in the same industry, but their potential for future growth justifies their higher valuation.

The primary objective of growth investing is to generate long-term capital appreciation by investing in companies with the potential for above-average growth. Growth investors are typically less concerned with short-term fluctuations in stock price and more focused on the long-term potential for growth.

While all three investment strategies aim to generate returns for investors, they differ in their investment philosophies and objectives. Value investing is focused on buying undervalued stocks and holding them until they reach their intrinsic value, while dividend investing is focused on generating income from regular dividend payments. Growth investing is focused on investing in companies with the potential for above-average growth in earnings and revenue.

Value and dividend investing are often considered to be more conservative investment strategies, as they tend to focus on well-established, stable companies with a history of consistent profits and cash flow.

HOW TO BUILD A DIVERSIFIED GROWTH PORTFOLIO

Building a diversified growth portfolio is an important step in achieving long-term investment success. A diversified portfolio can help investors minimize risk while maximizing returns by spreading investments across different asset classes, industries, and regions. In this chapter, we'll explore the key steps in building a diversified growth portfolio.

Step 1: Determine Your Investment Goals And Risk Tolerance

The first step in building a diversified growth

portfolio is to determine your investment goals and risk tolerance. Your investment goals will determine the type of investments you make, while your risk tolerance will determine the level of risk you are willing to take on.

For example, if your investment goal is long-term growth and you have a high risk tolerance, you may choose to invest in growth stocks or emerging markets. On the other hand, if your investment goal is income and you have a low risk tolerance, you may choose to invest in bonds or dividend-paying stocks.

Step 2: Choose Your Asset Allocation

The next step in building a diversified growth portfolio is to choose your asset allocation. Asset allocation is the process of dividing your investments among different assets, such as stocks, gold, bonds, and cash. Your asset allocation will depend on your investment goals, investing timeline, and risk tolerance.

A common asset allocation for a growth portfolio is 80% stocks and 20% bonds. This allocation provides exposure to the potential growth of stocks while minimizing risk through the inclusion of bonds.

Step 3: Invest In Different Industries And Regions

The next step in building a diversified growth portfolio is to invest in different industries and regions. Investing in different industries can help reduce the risk of having all your investments in one industry that may be subject to market fluctuations or changes in consumer behavior.

Investing in different regions can also help reduce risk by spreading investments across different economies and political climates. For example, investing in emerging markets can provide exposure to the potential growth of these economies while minimizing risk through diversification.

Step 4: Invest In Different Types Of Assets

The final step in building a diversified growth portfolio is to invest in different types of assets. This can include stocks, gold, bonds, real estate, commodities, and other investments. Investing in different types of assets can help reduce risk by providing exposure to different types of economic environments.

For example, investing in real estate can provide exposure to the potential growth of the real estate market while providing diversification away from traditional stocks and bonds.

Building a diversified growth portfolio is an important step in achieving long-term investment success. By determining your investment goals and risk tolerance, choosing your asset allocation, investing in different industries and regions, and investing in different types of assets, you can create a portfolio that maximizes returns while minimizing risk. It's important to regularly review and adjust your portfolio as your investment goals and risk tolerance change over time. As with any investment strategy, it's important to do your research and consult with a financial advisor before making any investment decisions.

STRATEGIES FOR MANAGING RISK AND VOLATILITY IN INVESTING

Growth investing can be a rewarding investment strategy, but it comes with its own unique set of risks and volatility. Fortunately, there are several strategies that investors can use to manage risk and volatility while still pursuing growth investments. In this chapter, we'll explore some of the most effective strategies for managing risk and volatility in growth investing.

1. Diversification

Diversification as we mentioned previously, is one of the most effective strategies for managing risk and volatility in growth investing. By diversifying your portfolio across different industries, regions, and asset classes, you can reduce your exposure to any one particular risk. This can help minimize the impact of market fluctuations and prevent any one loss from having a significant impact on your overall portfolio.

2. Asset Allocation

Asset allocation is another important strategy for managing risk and volatility in growth investing. By allocating your investments across different asset classes, such as stocks, bonds, and cash, you can reduce your exposure to any one particular risk. For example, if you have a high risk tolerance, you may allocate a larger portion of your portfolio to stocks. However, if you have a lower risk tolerance, you may allocate a larger portion of your portfolio to bonds.

3. Dollar Cost Averaging

Dollar cost averaging is a strategy that involves investing a fixed dollar amount at regular intervals over a long period of time. By using dollar cost averaging, you can reduce the impact of market volatility on your portfolio. This is because you are investing a fixed amount at regular intervals, regardless of market conditions. This can help you avoid making emotional decisions based on market fluctuations and stick to a disciplined investment strategy.

4. Stop-Loss Orders

Stop-loss orders are another strategy for managing risk and volatility in growth investing. A stop-loss order is an order to sell a stock when it reaches a certain price. By using a stop-loss order, you can limit your potential losses in the event of a market downturn. For example, if you own a stock that is trading at $100 per share and you set a stop-loss order at $90 per share, your shares will be automatically sold if the stock price falls to $90 per share.

5. Fundamental Analysis

Fundamental analysis is a strategy that involves analyzing a company's financials, competitive advantages, and growth prospects to determine its intrinsic value. By using fundamental analysis, you can identify companies with strong growth potential that are less likely to be impacted by market fluctuations. This can help you build a portfolio of growth stocks that are less vulnerable to market volatility.

Managing risk and volatility is an important part of growth investing. By using strategies such as diversification, asset allocation, dollar cost averaging, stop-loss orders, and fundamental analysis, you can minimize the impact of market fluctuations on your portfolio while still pursuing growth investments. It's important to regularly review and adjust your portfolio as your investment goals and risk tolerance change over time. As with any investment strategy, it's important to do your research and consult with a financial advisor before making any investment decisions.

WHAT ARE STOP LOSS ORDERS IN INVESTING?

S top loss orders are a type of order that investors can use to limit their potential losses when investing in the stock market. Stop loss orders are an effective tool for managing risk and can be used in conjunction with other investment strategies to minimize the impact of market volatility on a portfolio. In this chapter, we'll explore what stop loss orders are and how they can be used in investing.

What Are Stop Loss Orders?

A stop loss order is an order to sell a stock when it reaches a certain price. Stop loss orders are typically used to limit potential losses in the event of a market downturn or unexpected news that may impact the value of a stock. For example, if an investor owns a stock that is trading at $100 per share, they may set a stop loss order at $90 per share. If the stock price falls to $90 per share, the investor's shares will be automatically sold, limiting their potential losses.

The Types of Stop Loss Orders

There are several types of stop loss orders that investors can use, including:

1. Market Stop Loss Order: A market stop loss order is an order to sell a stock when it reaches a certain price, regardless of the market conditions. This type of order is executed at the next available price after the stop price is reached.

2. Limit Stop Loss Order: A limit stop loss order is an order to sell a stock when it reaches a certain price, but only if that price can be obtained. This type of order is executed at the limit price or better after the stop price is reached.

3. Trailing Stop Loss Order: A trailing stop loss order is an order to sell a stock when it falls a certain percentage from its highest point. This type of order is often used in volatile markets, as it allows investors to capture gains while limiting potential losses.

Benefits of Using Stop Loss Orders

Stop loss orders are an effective tool for managing risk and can be used in conjunction with other investment strategies to minimize the impact of market volatility on a portfolio. The benefits of using stop loss orders include:

1. Limiting Potential Losses: Stop loss orders can help limit potential losses in the event of a market downturn or unexpected news that may impact the value of a stock.

2. Removing Emotion from Investing: Stop loss orders can help remove emotion from investing by automating the process of selling stocks at a predetermined price.

3. Flexibility: Stop loss orders can be customized to fit an investor's specific needs, including the type of order, the stop price, and the limit price.

Stop loss orders are an effective tool for managing risk and can be used in conjunction with other investment strategies to minimize the impact of market volatility on a portfolio. By automating the process of selling stocks at a predetermined price, stop loss orders can help remove emotion from investing and limit potential losses. As with any investment strategy, it's important to do your research and consult with a financial advisor before making any investment decisions.

HOW TO MONITOR AND REBALANCE YOUR PORTFOLIO OVER TIME

Y ou've taken the time to establish an asset allocation strategy that fits your investment goals and risk tolerance. However, at the end of the year, you may find that the weighting of each asset class in your portfolio has shifted. What could have caused this?

Throughout the year, the market value of each security in your portfolio may have earned a different return, leading to changes in weighting. To address this, investors may turn to portfolio rebalancing - a process that involves adjusting the weightings of assets in an investment portfolio. This is similar to getting a tune-up for your car: it enables investors to keep their risk levels in check and reduce risk.

Rebalancing involves adjusting the weightings of different asset classes within a portfolio by buying or selling portions of the holdings. The aim is to restore the original proportions of each asset class in the portfolio. Additionally, if an investor's investment strategy or risk tolerance has changed, they can use rebalancing to readjust the weightings of each security or asset class to fulfill a newly devised asset allocation. By doing so, investors can ensure that their portfolio aligns with their investment goals and risk tolerance, helping to minimize risk and maximize returns.

As a result of varying returns among securities and asset classes, the asset mix that an investor initially created will inevitably change over time. This means that the percentage allocated to each asset class will shift accordingly.

However, these changes can increase or decrease the risk of the portfolio. Therefore, it's important to compare a rebalanced portfolio to one where changes were ignored. We must also examine the potential consequences of neglected allocations in a portfolio.

Example

Let's consider a growth portfolio consisting of three assets: a technology stock fund, a healthcare stock fund, and a renewable energy stock fund. Initially, the portfolio is allocated as follows:

- 40% in the technology stock fund

- 30% in the healthcare stock fund

- 30% in the renewable energy stock fund

Over the course of a year, the technology stock fund experiences significant growth, resulting in a weighting of 50% in the portfolio. The healthcare stock fund and the renewable energy stock fund, on the other hand, have underperformed, resulting in weightings of 25% and 25%, respectively.

To rebalance the portfolio, the investor would need to sell a portion of the technology stock fund and use the proceeds to buy additional shares of the healthcare and renewable energy stock funds. The goal is to bring the portfolio back to its original asset allocation of 40% technology, 30% healthcare, and 30% renewable energy.

Assuming the portfolio's total value is $100,000, the rebalancing process might look something like this:

- Sell $10,000 worth of shares in the technology stock fund (50% of the $20,000 invested) to reduce the weighting to 40%.

- Use the $10,000 to purchase additional shares in the healthcare and renewable energy stock funds, allocating $5,000 to each fund to bring their weightings up to 35%.

By rebalancing the portfolio in this way, the investor can ensure that their growth portfolio stays on track with their investment goals and risk tolerance, while minimizing risk and maximizing returns. It's important to note that rebalancing should be done regularly, as changes in asset values can quickly alter a portfolio's weighting and risk level.

INVESTING STRATEGIES FOR DIFFERENT TYPES OF GROWTH STOCKS

I nvesting in growth stocks can be a lucrative way to build wealth over the long term, but not all growth stocks are created equal. Different types of growth stocks have unique characteristics, requiring different investment strategies to achieve optimal returns. In this chapter, we'll explore the various types of growth stocks and the investment strategies that are best suited for each.

1. Emerging Growth Stocks

Emerging growth stocks are companies that are in

the early stages of their growth trajectory and have the potential to experience rapid growth in the future. These companies may be in new markets or have innovative products or services that have yet to be fully adopted by consumers.

Investment strategy: When investing in emerging growth stocks, it's important to focus on the company's potential for future growth. Look for companies with strong leadership, innovative products or services, and a sizable addressable market. These stocks tend to be more volatile, so it's important to keep an eye on risk management strategies like stop-loss orders and diversification.

2. Blue-Chip Growth Stocks

Blue-chip growth stocks are companies that have a proven track record of delivering steady growth over time. These companies may be industry leaders with well-established brands and a long history of successful operations.

Investment strategy: When investing in blue-chip growth stocks, it's important to focus on the company's long-term performance rather than short-term market fluctuations. These stocks tend to be less volatile than emerging growth stocks, making them a good choice for more conservative investors. However, it's important to keep an eye on valuations and avoid overpaying for these stocks.

3. Momentum Growth Stocks

Momentum growth stocks are companies that have recently experienced strong price momentum, typically over the past 6 to 12 months. These companies may be experiencing a surge in investor interest due to positive news or a strong earnings report.

Investment strategy: When investing in momentum growth stocks, it's important to be aware of the risks of buying into a stock that has already experienced a significant price increase. Look for companies with strong fundamentals that can sustain their growth over the long term. Set a stop-loss order to minimize risk if the stock's price begins to decline.

4. Dividend Growth Stocks

Dividend growth stocks are companies that have a history of paying and increasing dividends to shareholders over time. These companies may be well-established and profitable, with a strong track record of generating steady cash flow.

Investment strategy: When investing in dividend growth stocks, it's important to focus on the company's dividend history and cash flow generation. Look for companies with a history of steady dividend increases and a solid balance sheet. These stocks tend to be less volatile than other growth stocks, making them a good choice for income-oriented investors.

5. Cyclical Growth Stocks

Cyclical growth stocks are companies that are tied to the performance of the overall economy. These companies may be in industries like construction, manufacturing, or travel and leisure that tend to do well when the economy is strong.

Investment strategy: When investing in cyclical growth stocks, it's important to be aware of the risks of investing in companies that are tied to the economy's performance. Look for companies with a strong competitive position in their industry and a history of successful operations during economic downturns. Keep an eye on the economic indicators that impact the company's performance, such as interest rates and consumer spending.

Investing in growth stocks requires a careful consideration of the different types of growth stocks and the investment strategies that are best suited for each. By focusing on the unique characteristics of each type of growth stock, investors can build a diversified portfolio that maximizes returns while minimizing risk.

HOW TO INVEST IN GROWTH-ORIENTED ETFS

Exchange-traded funds (ETFs) are a popular investment vehicle that have grown in popularity over the past few decades. ETFs are similar to mutual funds in that they allow investors to pool their money together to invest in a diversified portfolio of stocks, bonds, or other assets. However, ETFs are traded on an exchange like individual stocks, providing investors with greater flexibility and lower costs than traditional mutual funds. In this chapter, we'll explore the basics of ETFs and how they work.

What is an ETF?

An ETF is a type of investment fund that tracks the performance of a specific index or group of assets. ETFs are designed to provide investors with exposure to a diversified portfolio of assets in a single investment vehicle. ETFs can be composed of stocks, bonds, commodities, or other types of assets.

How do ETFs work?

ETFs are traded on stock exchanges like individual stocks, allowing investors to buy and sell them throughout the trading day. The value of an ETF is determined by the underlying assets in the fund, and the price of the ETF can fluctuate throughout the day based on supply and demand.

ETFs are typically passively managed, meaning that they track the performance of a specific index or group of assets, rather than trying to beat the market through active management. This passive approach allows ETFs to offer lower costs and greater transparency than traditional mutual funds.

What are the benefits of investing in ETFs?

There are several benefits of investing in ETFs, including:

1. Diversification: ETFs provide investors with exposure to a diversified portfolio of assets in a single investment vehicle, reducing risk and volatility.

2. Lower costs: ETFs tend to have lower fees and expenses than traditional mutual funds, making them a cost-effective way to invest.

3. Flexibility: ETFs can be bought and sold like individual stocks, providing investors with greater flexibility than traditional mutual funds.

4. Transparency: ETFs are designed to track specific indexes or groups of assets, providing investors with greater transparency than actively managed mutual funds.

5. Tax efficiency: ETFs tend to be more tax-efficient than traditional mutual funds, reducing the impact of taxes on investment returns.

What are the risks of investing in ETFs?

While ETFs offer many benefits, there are also risks to consider, including:

1. Market risk: ETFs are subject to the same market risk as individual stocks and other investments.

2. Tracking error: ETFs may not perfectly track the performance of their underlying index or assets, resulting in a tracking error.

3. Liquidity risk: Some ETFs may be less liquid than others, making it difficult to buy or sell shares at a fair price.

4. Concentration risk: Some ETFs may be heavily concentrated in a particular sector

or asset, increasing the risk of losses in that area.

Examples of Growth ETFs (with their ticker symbols in brackets and expense ratios)

Please note this information is correct at the time of writing.

Vanguard Growth ETF (VUG)	0.04%
iShares Morningstar Mid-Cap Growth ETF (IMCG)	0.06%
Vanguard S&P Small-Cap 600 Growth ETF (VIOG)	0.15%
Nuveen ESG Large-Cap Growth ETF (NULG)	0.25%
Direxion NASDAQ-100 Equal Weight ETF (QQQE)	0.35%
Vanguard U.S. Momentum Factor ETF (VFMO)	0.13%
Vanguard International Dividend Appreciation ETF (VIGI)	0.15%

ETFs are a popular investment vehicle that offer investors a low-cost, diversified way to invest in a specific index or group of assets. ETFs can provide many benefits, including lower costs, greater flexibility, and tax efficiency. However, investors should also be aware of the risks of investing in ETFs, including market risk, tracking error, liquidity risk, and concentration risk.

UNDERSTANDING OPTIONS AND DERIVATIVES TO ENHANCE RETURNS

Options and derivatives are financial instruments that can be used by investors to manage risk, hedge positions, and enhance returns. While they can be complex, understanding the basics of options and derivatives is essential for any investor who wishes to utilize them in their portfolio.

Options

Call and put options are two types of options that are commonly used by investors to manage risk, hedge positions, and enhance returns. Understanding the differences between these two options is essential for any investor who wishes to utilize them in their portfolio.

A call option is a contract that gives the holder the right, but not the obligation, to buy an underlying asset at a specific price and time. The buyer of a call option is said to have a long call position, while the seller of a call option is said to have a short call position.

The price at which the underlying asset can be bought is known as the strike price, while the date on which the option expires is known as the expiration date. Call options can be purchased on a variety of underlying assets, including stocks, bonds, commodities, and currencies.

Investors typically purchase call options when they believe that the price of the underlying asset will increase. If the price of the underlying asset does increase, the holder of the call option can exercise the option and buy the asset at the lower strike price, then immediately sell the asset at the higher market price, realizing a profit.

A put option is a contract that gives the holder the right, but not the obligation, to sell an underlying asset at a specific price and time. The buyer of a put option is said to have a long put position, while the seller of a put option is said to have a short put position.

As with call options, the strike price and expiration date are specified in the put option contract. Put options can be purchased on a variety of underlying assets, including stocks, bonds, commodities, and currencies.

Investors typically purchase put options when they believe that the price of the underlying asset will decrease. If the price of the underlying asset does decrease, the holder of the put option can exercise the option and sell the asset at the higher strike price, then immediately buy the asset at the lower market price, realizing a profit.

While call-and-put options can be purchased by investors, they can also be sold by investors. Selling options can be a way for investors to generate income, but it also exposes them to potentially unlimited losses.

When an investor sells a call option, they are said to have a short call position. If the price of the underlying asset increases and the holder of the call option exercises the option, the investor who sold the option will be required to sell the asset at the lower strike price, resulting in a loss.

When an investor sells a put option, they are said to have a short put position. If the price of the underlying asset decreases and the holder of the put option exercises the option, the investor who sold the option will be required to buy the asset at the higher strike price, resulting in a loss.

Call and put options are powerful tools that can be used by investors to manage risk, hedge positions, and enhance returns. Understanding the differences between these two types of options is essential for any investor who wishes to utilize them in their portfolio. It is important to carefully consider the risks and potential rewards of using call and put options before implementing them in a portfolio.

Derivatives

Derivatives refer to financial instruments whose value is determined by the underlying asset, which could be a commodity or a stock, among others. Derivatives are commonly used in stock investing to manage risk, hedge positions, and enhance returns. Understanding the different types of derivatives is essential for any investor who wishes to utilize them in their portfolio.

Futures contracts are a type of derivative that obligate the buyer to purchase an underlying asset at a specific price and time in the future. Futures contracts can be purchased on a variety of underlying assets, including stocks, bonds, commodities, and currencies.

Futures contracts can be used by investors to hedge their positions in the underlying asset. For example, an investor who owns a stock could purchase a futures contract on the stock to lock in a price and protect against a decline in the stock price.

Futures contracts can also be used by investors to speculate on the direction of the underlying asset. For example, an investor who believes that the price of a commodity will increase could purchase a futures contract on the commodity, hoping to profit from the price increase.

Swaps are another type of derivative that involve the exchange of cash flows between two parties. Swaps can be used to manage risk or to speculate on the direction of interest rates, currencies, or other financial variables.

For example, a company that has borrowed money at a variable interest rate could enter into an interest rate swap with another party to exchange their variable rate payments for fixed rate payments. This would protect the company against an increase in interest rates.

Derivatives are powerful tools that can be used by investors to manage risk, hedge positions, and enhance returns. Understanding the different types of derivatives is essential for any investor who wishes to utilize them in their portfolio. It is important to carefully consider the risks and potential rewards of using derivatives before implementing them in a portfolio.

KEY METRICS TO CONSIDER WHEN ANALYZING GROWTH STOCKS

When it comes to analyzing growth stocks, there are a variety of key metrics that investors should consider. These metrics can help investors evaluate a company's financial health, growth potential, and overall performance. In this chapter, we will explore some of the most important metrics to consider when analyzing growth stocks.

Revenue Growth Rate

1. One of the most important metrics to consider when evaluating growth stocks is revenue growth rate. This metric tells you how much a company's revenue has increased over a certain period of time. Companies that are growing quickly will typically have a higher revenue growth rate. It's important to look at both the current

revenue growth rate and the historical trend to determine if a company is on a sustained growth trajectory.

Earnings Growth Rate

2. Earnings growth rate is another important metric to consider when analyzing growth stocks. This metric tells you how much a company's earnings have grown over a certain period of time. A company's earnings growth rate is a good indicator of its profitability and its ability to generate returns for investors. Like revenue growth rate, it's important to look at both the current earnings growth rate and the historical trend.

Price-to-Earnings Ratio (P/E Ratio)

3. The price-to-earnings ratio, or P/E ratio, is a valuation metric that compares a company's current stock price to its earnings per share (EPS). This metric is often used to evaluate whether a company's stock is overvalued or undervalued. Companies with high P/E ratios are often considered growth stocks because investors are willing to pay a premium for their earnings growth potential.

Price-to-Sales Ratio (P/S Ratio)

4. The price-to-sales ratio, or P/S ratio, is

another valuation metric that compares a company's current stock price to its revenue per share. This metric is often used to evaluate growth stocks because it can help investors determine if a company's current stock price is justified based on its revenue growth potential.

Gross Margin

5. Gross margin is a measure of a company's profitability that compares its revenue to its cost of goods sold (COGS). Companies with high gross margins are often considered more valuable because they are able to generate more profit from their sales. Gross margin is an important metric to consider when analyzing growth stocks because it can give investors an idea of a company's ability to scale its business and generate consistent profits.

Return on Equity (ROE)

6. Return on equity, or ROE, is a measure of a company's profitability that compares its net income to its shareholder equity. This metric is often used to evaluate how well a company is using its shareholders' investments to generate profits. Companies with high ROE are often considered more valuable because they are able to generate more profits from each dollar of

shareholder equity.

Debt-to-Equity Ratio

7. The debt-to-equity ratio is a measure of a company's financial leverage that compares its total debt to its shareholder equity. This metric can help investors evaluate a company's financial health and its ability to pay back its debts. Companies with high debt-to-equity ratios may be riskier investments, but they may also have higher growth potential if they are able to effectively manage their debt.

When it comes to analyzing growth stocks, there are a variety of key metrics that investors should consider. By evaluating a company's revenue growth rate, earnings growth rate, P/E ratio, P/S ratio, gross margin, ROE, and debt-to-equity ratio, investors can get a more complete picture of a company's financial health, growth potential, and overall performance. While no single metric can predict the future success of a company,

HOW TO INTERPRET FINANCIAL STATEMENTS AND OTHER DATA

Understanding a company's financial health is a crucial skill for aspiring investors, entrepreneurs, and managers. With this knowledge, investors can identify promising opportunities while managing risks, and professionals can make more strategic business decisions.

Financial statements provide valuable insight into a company's health, which may not be easily discernible through other methods. However, many business professionals lack the necessary training to interpret these documents, leading to obscured information.

If you are unfamiliar with financial statements, this guide can assist you in comprehending and analyzing the data they contain.

In order to comprehend a company's financial position, both independently and within its industry, it is necessary to examine and assess several financial statements, including balance sheets, income statements, cash flow statements, and annual reports. The significance of these documents lies in the narrative they present when examined in tandem.

How To Read A Balance Sheet

A balance sheet presents the "book value" of a company by providing a snapshot of its available resources and financing as of a specific date. It outlines the company's assets, liabilities, and owners' equity, which essentially indicates its debts, assets, and the amount invested by shareholders.

Moreover, the balance sheet offers valuable information that can be used to calculate rates of return and assess capital structure, through the use of the accounting equation: Assets = Liabilities + Owners' Equity.

Assets are tangible or intangible resources owned by

a company that hold measurable value.

Liabilities refer to a company's outstanding debts to creditors, including unpaid payroll expenses, debt payments, rent and utility bills, bonds payable, and taxes.

Owners' equity represents the overall net worth of a company, calculated by subtracting total liabilities from total assets. This amount of money is owned by the shareholders, who may include private owners or public investors.

However, the balance sheet alone does not provide information on financial trends, which is why it is necessary to review other financial statements, such as income and cash flow statements, to gain an insight into the company's financial position.

How To Read An Income Statement

An income statement, also referred to as a profit and loss (P&L) statement, provides a summary of the cumulative impact of revenue, expenses, gains, and losses over a specified period. This statement is frequently included in quarterly and annual reports and reveals financial trends, business operations (such as revenue and expenses), and comparisons over specific periods.

Typically, an income statement will contain the following information:

- Revenue: The total amount of money a

business earns

- Expenses: The total amount of money a business spends

- Cost of Goods Sold (COGS): The cost of producing the goods or services that a business sells

- Gross Profit: Total revenue minus COGS

- Operating Income: Gross profit minus operating expenses

- Income before Taxes: Operating income minus non-operating expenses

- Net Income: Income before taxes minus taxes

- Earnings per Share (EPS): The division of net income by the total number of outstanding shares

- Depreciation: The decrease in value of assets, such as equipment, over time

- EBITDA: Earnings (before interest, taxes, depreciation, and amortization)

How To Read A Cash Flow Statement

The purpose of a cash flow statement is to present a detailed overview of a business's cash movements during a specific period known as the accounting period. This statement shows how much cash is coming in and going out of the business and provides insight into the organization's short-term and long-term financial stability.

Cash flow statements are divided into three sections: cash flow from operating activities, cash flow from investing activities, and cash flow from financing activities. Operating activities reveal cash flow generated by a company's core goods or services, which includes both revenue and expenses. Investing activities represent cash flow from purchasing or selling assets using free cash instead of debt. Financing activities detail cash flow from debt and equity financing.

It is essential to understand the distinction between cash flow and profit. While cash flow represents the cash that is moving in and out of a company, profit refers to what remains after all expenses have been subtracted from revenues. Both are critical figures to consider.

A cash flow statement allows you to identify the types of activities that generate cash and make informed financial decisions. Ideally, cash from operating income should exceed net income consistently, as positive cash flow indicates a company's financial stability and growth potential. However, having a positive cash flow does not always equate to profitability, which is why analyzing balance sheets and income statements is also important.

How To Read An Annual Report

An annual report is a mandatory publication that publicly traded corporations must issue to shareholders on an annual basis. It describes the company's financial and operational conditions.

Annual reports frequently incorporate editorial content, including images, infographics, and a letter from the CEO, to communicate corporate activities, achievements, and benchmarks. They provide investors, shareholders, and employees with a deeper understanding of the company's mission and goals compared to individual financial statements.

Aside from editorial content, an annual report summarizes financial data and includes the company's income statement, balance sheet, and cash flow statement. It also provides industry insights, management's discussion and analysis (MD&A). Also accounting policies, and additional investor information.

In addition to an annual report, the US Securities and Exchange Commission (SEC) mandates public companies to issue a more detailed 10-K report. The 10-K report provides investors with a comprehensive view of a company's financial status before they buy or sell shares. It is organized in accordance with SEC guidelines and includes detailed descriptions of the company's financial activity, corporate agreements, risks, opportunities, current operations, executive compensation, and market activity. Additionally, the 10-K report features a detailed discussion of operations for the year and a thorough analysis of the industry and marketplace.

Both the annual report and 10-K report offer valuable insight into a company's financial health, status, and goals. While the annual report may provide a narrative element, including management's vision for the company, the 10-K report offers additional detail to reinforce and expand upon that narrative.

EVALUATING
A COMPANY'S
MANAGEMENT
TEAM AND
COMPETITIVE
POSITION

E valuating a company's management team and competitive position is critical for investors and stakeholders to make informed decisions about the company's prospects and potential for long-term success. This chapter will discuss the key factors to consider when assessing a company's management team and competitive position.

Assessing the Management Team

One of the most important factors in evaluating a company's potential for success is the quality of its management team. Here are some factors to consider:

1. Experience and Qualifications: Look for a management team with relevant industry experience and strong educational backgrounds. An experienced management team with a track record of success is a positive indicator of a company's future prospects.

2. Leadership Style: Assess the management team's leadership style and values to determine if they align with the company's culture and goals. A strong management team should be able to inspire and motivate employees to work towards the company's objectives.

3. Succession Planning: Look for a management team with a clear plan for succession in the event of retirement or unforeseen circumstances. A solid succession plan will ensure that the company continues to operate smoothly and maintain its momentum.

4. Communication: Communication is key in any successful organization. Assess the management team's communication skills

and ensure they are transparent and open with stakeholders.

Assessing Competitive Position

Evaluating a company's competitive position involves analyzing its market share, industry trends, and competitive landscape. Here are some factors to consider:

1. Market Share: Analyze the company's market share to determine its position within the industry. A company with a strong market share is likely to have a competitive advantage over its rivals.

2. Industry Trends: Keep up-to-date with industry trends to ensure the company is keeping pace with emerging technologies and market developments. A company that is slow to adapt to new trends risks falling behind its competitors.

3. Competitive Landscape: Analyze the competitive landscape to determine the company's strengths and weaknesses. Assess the company's ability to differentiate itself from its competitors and identify any potential threats to its market share.

4. Financial Health: Assess the company's financial health to determine its ability to compete effectively in the marketplace. Look for a company with a strong balance

sheet and healthy cash flow to fund growth and invest in new technologies.

Evaluating a company's management team and competitive position is critical for investors and stakeholders to make informed decisions. A strong management team with relevant industry experience and a clear plan for succession is essential for long-term success. An understanding of the competitive landscape, market share, and industry trends is also necessary to determine a company's potential for growth and profitability. By assessing these key factors, investors and stakeholders can gain a deeper understanding of a company's prospects and make informed decisions about their investments.

HOW TO CALCULATE RETURN ON EQUITY (ROE)

Return on Equity (ROE) is a financial ratio that measures the profitability of a company in relation to its shareholders' equity. ROE is a useful metric for investors to evaluate a company's financial health and profitability. In this chapter, we will discuss how to calculate ROE and what it tells us about a company's performance.

Step 1: Determine Shareholders' Equity

The first step in calculating ROE is to determine the shareholders' equity. Shareholders' equity is the difference between the company's assets and liabilities. It represents the amount of money that would be left over if a company sold all of its assets and paid off all of its debts.

The formula for shareholders' equity is:

Shareholders' Equity = Total Assets - Total Liabilities

Step 2: Calculate Net Income

The second step in calculating ROE is to determine the net income of the company. Net income is the profit that a company earns after subtracting all of its expenses, taxes, and interest payments from its revenue.

The formula for net income is:

Net Income = Total Revenue - Total Expenses - Taxes - Interest

Step 3: Calculate Return on Equity

Once you have determined the shareholders' equity and net income, you can calculate the return on equity (ROE) using the following formula:

ROE = Net Income / Shareholders' Equity

ROE is expressed as a percentage. A higher ROE indicates that a company is more profitable and generating more returns for its shareholders. A lower ROE indicates that a company is less profitable and generating fewer returns for its shareholders.

ROE is an important metric for investors to evaluate a company's financial health and profitability. A high ROE is generally seen as a positive sign, as it indicates that the company is using its shareholders' equity effectively to generate profits. However, a high ROE can also indicate that a company is taking on too much risk or is using excessive leverage.

On the other hand, a low ROE may indicate that a company is not generating enough profits relative to its shareholders' equity. However, a low ROE can also be the result of a company reinvesting its profits back into the business to fund growth opportunities.

ROE is a useful metric for investors to evaluate a company's financial health and profitability. Calculating ROE involves determining the shareholders' equity and net income of the company and using these figures to calculate the ratio. A high ROE indicates that a company is more profitable and generating more returns for its shareholders, while a low ROE may indicate that a company is not generating enough profits relative to its shareholders' equity.

HOW TO CALCULATE EARNINGS PER SHARE (EPS)

Earnings Per Share (EPS) is a financial ratio that measures the company's profitability on a per-share basis. EPS is a commonly used metric for evaluating the financial performance of a company and is an important factor that investors consider when making investment decisions. In this chapter, we will discuss how to calculate EPS and what it tells us about a company's financial health.

Step 1: Determine Net Income

The first step in calculating EPS is to determine the net income of the company. Net income is the profit that a company earns after subtracting all of its expenses, taxes, and interest payments from its revenue.

The formula for net income is:

Net Income = Total Revenue - Total Expenses - Taxes - Interest

Step 2: Calculate Weighted Average Number Of Shares

The second step in calculating EPS is to determine the weighted average number of shares outstanding during the period. This takes into account any changes in the number of shares outstanding during the period, such as stock issuances or repurchases.

The formula for weighted average number of shares is:

Weighted Average Number of Shares = (Beginning Number of Shares + Ending Number of Shares) / 2

Step 3: Calculate Earnings Per Share

Once you have determined the net income and weighted average number of shares outstanding, you can calculate EPS using the following formula:

EPS = Net Income / Weighted Average Number of Shares

EPS is expressed as a dollar amount per share. A higher EPS indicates that a company is more profitable on a per-share basis, while a lower EPS indicates that a company is less profitable on a per-share basis.

EPS is an important metric for investors to evaluate a company's financial health and profitability. A higher EPS is generally seen as a positive sign, as it indicates that the company is generating more profits per share for its shareholders. However, a high EPS can also be the result of a company repurchasing its own shares, which can inflate the EPS figure.

On the other hand, a lower EPS may indicate that a company is not generating as much profit per share for its shareholders. However, a low EPS can also be the result of a company reinvesting its profits back into the business to fund growth opportunities.

EPS is a useful metric for investors to evaluate a company's financial health and profitability on a per-share basis. Calculating EPS involves determining the net income of the company and the weighted average number of shares outstanding during the period and using these figures to calculate the ratio. A higher EPS indicates that a company is generating more profits per share for its shareholders, while a lower EPS may indicate that a company is not generating as much profit per share for its shareholders.

DOLLAR COST AVERAGING FOR INVESTING: A STRATEGY FOR LONG-TERM SUCCESS

Dollar cost averaging (DCA) is an investment strategy that involves investing a fixed dollar amount at regular intervals over a long period of time. DCA can be an effective strategy for long-term investors who are looking to build a diversified investment portfolio while minimizing risk. In this chapter, we'll explore the benefits of dollar cost averaging and provide examples of how it works.

The Benefits of Dollar Cost Averaging

One of the primary benefits of dollar cost averaging is that it helps investors avoid the temptation to time the market. Timing the market involves trying to buy stocks at the lowest possible price and sell them at the highest possible price. This is a difficult strategy to execute successfully, as it requires investors to accurately predict market movements.

Dollar cost averaging eliminates the need to time the market, as investors are investing a fixed dollar amount at regular intervals regardless of market conditions. This can help investors avoid emotional decision-making and stick to a disciplined investment strategy.

Dollar cost averaging can also help investors build a diversified investment portfolio over time. By investing a fixed dollar amount at regular intervals, investors can purchase shares of different stocks and funds at various prices, which can help reduce overall portfolio risk.

Example of Dollar Cost Averaging

Let's say that you have $12,000 to invest in the stock market. Instead of investing the entire amount at once, you decide to use dollar cost averaging to invest $1,000 per month over the course of one year.

Month 1: Invest $1,000 in Fund A at $10 per share, purchasing 100 shares

Month 2: Invest $1,000 in Fund A at $12 per share, purchasing 83 shares

Month 3: Invest $1,000 in Fund B at $15 per share, purchasing 67 shares

Month 4: Invest $1,000 in Fund C at $18 per share, purchasing 56 shares

Month 5: Invest $1,000 in Fund B at $16 per share, purchasing 63 shares

Month 6: Invest $1,000 in Fund A at $11 per share, purchasing 91 shares

Month 7: Invest $1,000 in Fund C at $20 per share, purchasing 50 shares

Month 8: Invest $1,000 in Fund B at $14 per share, purchasing 71 shares

Month 9: Invest $1,000 in Fund A at $13 per share, purchasing 77 shares

Month 10: Invest $1,000 in Fund C at $17 per share, purchasing 59 shares

Month 11: Invest $1,000 in Fund B at $13 per share, purchasing 77 shares

Month 12: Invest $1,000 in Fund A at $12 per share, purchasing 83 shares

At the end of the year, you have invested a total of $12,000 and own shares in three different funds. By using dollar cost averaging, you have purchased shares at various prices, which can help reduce portfolio risk. If you had invested the entire $12,000 at once, you may have purchased all of your shares at a higher price, which could have negatively impacted your returns.

Dollar cost averaging can be an effective investment strategy for long-term investors who are looking to build a diversified portfolio while minimizing risk. By investing a fixed dollar amount at regular intervals, investors can avoid the temptation to time the market and make emotional decisions. Dollar cost averaging can also help investors build a diversified portfolio over time, which can help reduce overall portfolio risk.

CONCLUSION

Growth investing is an investment strategy that focuses on investing in companies that have the potential for significant growth in the future. In this chapter, we will recap the key takeaways of growth investing.

1. Look for companies with strong growth potential

When selecting companies for a growth investment strategy, it is important to look for companies with strong growth potential. This may include companies that are in emerging markets, companies that are developing new technologies or products, or companies that are in industries that are expected to experience significant growth in the future.

2. Analyze financial statements and metrics

When evaluating companies for a growth investment strategy, it is important to analyze the company's financial statements and metrics. This includes metrics such as revenue growth, earnings growth, return on equity (ROE), and earnings per share (EPS). These metrics can help investors identify companies that are experiencing strong growth and are likely to continue to grow in the future.

3. Consider the company's competitive advantage

When selecting companies for a growth investment strategy, it is important to consider the company's competitive advantage. This may include the company's brand, intellectual property, or unique business model. Companies with a strong competitive advantage are more likely to succeed in the long term and experience strong growth.

4. Diversify your portfolio

As with any investment strategy, it is important to diversify your portfolio when investing in growth stocks. This can help reduce risk and ensure that your portfolio is not overly exposed to any one company or industry.

5. Be patient

Investing in growth stocks requires patience. Companies with strong growth potential may take time to realize their full potential, and there may be periods of volatility in the stock price. It is important to have a long-term perspective when investing in growth stocks and to be willing to ride out any short-term fluctuations in the market.

Growth investing is an investment strategy that focuses on investing in companies with strong growth potential. When selecting companies for a growth investment strategy, it is important to analyze the company's financial statements and metrics, consider the company's competitive advantage, and diversify your portfolio. It is also important to be patient and have a long-term perspective when investing in growth stocks. By following these key takeaways, investors can successfully implement a growth investing strategy and potentially achieve strong returns over the long term.

ADDITIONAL RESOURCES FOR FURTHER LEARNING

1. "The Intelligent Investor" by Benjamin Graham - This classic book is a must-read for any investor and provides a comprehensive overview of value investing, which is closely related to growth investing.

2. "One Up on Wall Street" by Peter Lynch - In this book, legendary investor Peter Lynch shares his insights on how to identify growth stocks and beat the market.

3. "The Little Book of Common Sense Investing" by John C. Bogle - This book provides a simple and straightforward approach to investing, focusing on low-cost index funds and a long-term perspective.

4. Morningstar.com - Morningstar is a popular

investment research website that provides in-depth analysis of stocks and mutual funds, including growth stocks.

5. SeekingAlpha.com - Seeking Alpha is a website that provides news, analysis, and commentary on a variety of investment topics, including growth investing.

6. Investopedia.com - Investopedia is a comprehensive online resource for investing education, providing articles, tutorials, and courses on a wide range of investment topics, including growth investing.

By utilizing these resources, investors can gain a deeper understanding of growth investing and develop a successful investment strategy.

WORKS CITED

Yahoo Finance – stock market live, quotes, business & finance news, https://uk.finance.yahoo.com/. Accessed March 2023.

Morningstar | Empowering Investor Success, http://morningstar.com. Accessed 9 March 2023.

Seeking Alpha | Stock Market Analysis & Tools for Investors, http://seekingalpha.com. Accessed March 2023.

Bogle, John C. *The Little Book of Common Sense Investing: The Only Way to Guarantee Your Fair Share of Stock Market Returns*. Wiley, 2017.

Cheng, Marguerita. "Top Growth Stocks."

Investopedia, https://www.investopedia.com/investing/best-growth-stocks/. Accessed March 2023.

"Google Finance - Stock Market Prices, Real-time Quotes & Business News." *Google*, https://www.google.com/finance/?hl=en. Accessed March 2023.

Lynch, Peter, and John Rothchild. *One Up On Wall Street: How To Use What You Already Know To Make Money In The Market*. Simon & Schuster, 2000.

Park, Meeyeon. "Growth Stocks - Overview, Characteristics, Examples." *Corporate Finance Institute*, 20 February 2023, https://corporatefinanceinstitute.com/resources/capital-markets/growth-stocks/. Accessed March 2023.

Zweig, Jason, and Benjamin Graham. *The*

Intelligent Investor. Edited by Jason Zweig, HarperCollins, 2006.

DISCLAIMER

Disclaimer: The author of this book is not a licensed financial professional and the information contained within is not intended to be taken as financial advice. Investing in stocks and other securities carries a risk of loss. Please consult a licensed financial advisor and conduct your own research before making any investment decisions.

It is also important to consult with a tax professional when dealing with tax implications of investing, especially when it comes to reporting, as tax laws and rules may vary depending on the country or state and the circumstances.